Teach Us
to Pray

William Roberts

LIGUORI PUBLICATIONS
Liguori, Missouri 63057

Imprimi Potest:
Daniel L. Lowery, C.SS.R.
Provincial, St. Louis Province
Redemptorist Fathers
April 10, 1972

Imprimatur:
St. Louis, April 13, 1972
+ John J. Cardinal Carberry
Archbishop of St. Louis

Library of Congress Catalog Card Number: 72-81175

FOREWORD

Presently the Director of Religious Education in a Dayton, Ohio, parish, Dr. Roberts has acquired degrees in English from Fordham and a Doctorate in Religious Studies from Marquette. After years of teaching in the West, in the Midwest and in the East, he was appointed chairman of the Department of Religious Studies at Wheeling College in West Virginia. Throughout his life he has taken an active part in programs of adult religious education.

His experience in his chosen field has convinced him that all prayer needs a definite purpose. We cannot survive, we cannot change what must be changed in our lives unless we pray. Prayer, to him — as it was to Alphonsus, the Doctor of prayer — is absolutely necessary for salvation. It must be directed to the ordinary happenings of our daily lives. Here, Dr. Roberts is not just preaching pragmatism. He is a realist who understands the theory of prayer, and who knows how to put that theory into practice.

Teach Us to Pray examines the modern approach to the theology of prayer. Most of us know that we must pray, but the motives for doing so are not always quite clear to us. After some reflections on prayer in general, the author examines in particular the prayer of petition, the prayer of a suffering man, and our Lord's own prayer. His interesting insights on these particulars are well worth reading.

Perhaps the most telling part of the entire book is Robert's definition of prayer: man's response to God who is already speaking to man. So often we look on prayer as our initial contact with God. But the author shows quite clearly that when we speak to God in prayer we are responding to Him who began the conversation in the first place. That the Father is continually speaking to us is brought out in greater length in two other current Liguorian paperbacks: *The Story of Hope: The Nation, The Man, The Kingdom* by Ronald A. Sarno, S.J. and *This is the Word of the Lord* by John F. Craghan, C.SS.R.

When Roberts writes about the prayer of petition, once again he clears the air of misconceptions. This type of prayer is not just a signal of distress or a request for gifts. True prayer of petition involves worship of God and thanksgiving to Him. It implies a commitment on the part of man to explore the possible and to accept the Father's will. Here again the author offers a valuable insight: pray as if everything depends *both* on God and on ourselves, and work as if everything depends on God and on ourselves.

After an enlightening commentary on a model prayer from the Old Testament (Psalm 22), Dr. Roberts treats of our Lord's own prayer. Perhaps the most impressive part here is his treatment on the kingdom. We are pilgrims on the way to the final and perfect kingdom. Christ proclaimed that kingdom to the people of all times. We must work through Him, with Him and in Him to establish it firmly here on earth. It will be lived fully in the next world.

We do not change Christ by our prayer. Christ changes us. Acceptance of change demands perfect imitation of the Father. Like Father, like Son. Christ has taught us how to pray. And the Spirit inspires us to follow His divine example. We certainly are in good company when we are in communication with the Big Three.

Christopher Farrell, C.SS.R.
Editor, Liguorian Books

PROLOGUE

Once Christ was in a certain place praying, and when He had finished one of His disciples said, "Lord, teach us to pray, just as John taught his disciples" (Lk 11:1).[1] For almost two thousand years since, Christians have been making the same request, "teach us to pray." Too often the answers offered have failed to reflect the simplicity of Christ's response.

This small book is an effort to bring together some of the essential aspects of Christ's prayer as it is reflected in the New Testament, and to point out some of the implications of this for our own prayer in today's world.

Chapter one presents a general consideration of the prayer of Christ and some of the implications this has for our own prayer life. Chapter two considers the prayer of petition; and chapter three presents a reflection on Psalm 22, the prayer which Christ prayed in His dying moments and which continues to serve as a model for suffering man. The concluding chapter summarizes the theme of this book by a consideration of the Lord's Prayer.

---

[1] All Scripture quotations are from the *Jerusalem Bible.*

Chapter One

CHRISTIAN PRAYER: SOME REFLECTIONS

CHRISTIAN PRAYER:
SOME REFLECTIONS

Prayer is man's response to God
who is already speaking to man.

This definition of prayer may surprise many people. We have often tended to think of and speak about prayer as a matter of man trying to get God's attention. We express the hope that if we pray hard enough God will hear us. If things do not turn out the way we wish, we complain that God did not heed our prayer.

Prayer, however, does not depend on the initiative of man. As the Council of Orange made clear, man could not even desire to seek God, if God was not already communicating His grace to man. Prayer is not man's effort to get God concerned. God is already concerned (Mt 6:8). Nor is it the endeavor on man's part to get God's attention. Rather, it is God who is trying to get man's attention.

In prayer God is already communicating to man. He is addressing himself to the innermost depths of man's being.

He is leading man to an awareness of His personal presence, so that man may respond in faith and love.

This chapter elaborates on this aspect of prayer by first reflecting on the prayer of Christ, and then considering the implications for our own approach to prayer.

THE PRAYER OF CHRIST

Once prayer is understood as man's response to God who is already speaking to man, it can be seen that the whole life and work of Christ is prayer. Christ is praying not only when He is formally uttering words to His Father. All He does and says is prayer, for it is all a sign of His filial response to the Father.

In the New Testament view the most important characteristic of Christ is His special relationship with the Father. The Father and Christ are one (Jn 10:30; 17:21-22). "The Father is in me and I am in the Father" (Jn 10:38; also 14:11). All the Father has He has given to the Son. Christ, on His part, has been totally receptive (cf. Jn 16:15). The Father knows (Jn 10:15) and loves Christ (Jn 5:20; 10:17; 15:19; 17:23). Christ responds in love to the Father. He has come into the world because His Father has consecrated Him and sent

Him (Jn 8:18,29; 10:36). He shepherds the flock the Father has given Him (Jn 10:29). He does the works which He sees His Father doing (Jn 5:19-20; 10:25, 32, 37, 38; 14:10). He preaches what the Father has taught Him (Jn 8:28, 38; 14:10; 15:15).

Yet, the fact that Christ's entire dedication of himself is genuine prayer does not preclude the important place that periods of formal prayer have in His life. During His ministry there are frequent occasions when He goes aside and exclusively directs His attention to dialogue with His Father. After His baptism He is led by the Spirit into the wilderness for a forty-day period (Lk 4:1). When He has multiplied the loaves, He retreats from those who want to make Him king, and goes off by himself to pray (Mt 14:23; Jn 6:15). Before He chooses His twelve apostles, He spends the whole night out in the hills in prayer (Lk 6:12-13). It is His custom to get away and spend time on the Mount of Olives (Lk 22:39).

What is the nature of Christ's prayer? His prayer is one of thanksgiving. He expresses gratitude to His Father for revealing the good news to the little ones (Mt 11:25). He gives thanks to Him before He multiplies the loaves and fishes (Jn 6:11), when He raises Lazarus from the dead (Jn 11:41, 42), and as He shares the bread and cup at the Last Supper (Lk 22:17-20).

Christ's prayer to the Father is one of trust. He sees His Father as the one who feeds the birds in the sky, though they do not sow or reap or gather into barns. His Father is the one who adorns the flowers of the field with more splendor than Solomon in all his glory. This is a mere indication of the much greater concern and love the Father has for all mankind (Mt 6:26-31). It is with this kind of reliance on His Father's providence that Christ is able to entrust His life completely to the Father, even as He dies on the cross (Lk 23:46).

Finally, Christ's prayer is one of petition. He prays that His chosen ones be delivered from evil, and that they may be one as He and the Father are one (Jn 17:15, 21, ff.).

OUR APPROACH TO PRAYER

Taking as our starting point the simple definition of prayer — man's response to God who is already speaking to man — which is illustrated in our consideration of the prayer of Christ, we will develop some of the implications that this has for our own approach to prayer. Five areas will be treated here: a) the relationship between work and prayer; b) Christ as the center of Christian prayer; c) the essential element of prayer; d) simplification of prayer; e) shared prayer.

Work and Prayer

For the Christian there is often a tension between work and prayer. Some complain that they are so caught up in their work they have no time to pray. Others are tempted to sacrifice indispensable responsibilities in order to fit prayer into their life. Still others argue that since their work is prayer, there is no need to spend periods of time set aside exclusively for prayer.

The above definition of prayer can provide the key for resolving this tension. If prayer is man's response to a communicative God, then everything that man does in openness to God is prayer. This response is not just verbalized, it is lived. To the extent that a Christian pursues his life under the influence of Christ's Gospel he is praying, for he is responding in a living way to the dynamic Word of God. Every effort to relate to another in Christian love is a sign of one's personal acceptance of Christ, and so too is prayer. As

John tells us, if anyone says he loves God, but does not show this by love of neighbor, he is a liar (I Jn 4:20; cf. also 2:4, ff. and 3:17). Christ makes clear that what we do to others is what we do to Him (Mt 25:40, 45). It is not he who *says* "Lord, Lord" who enters the kingdom, but he who *does* the will of the Father (Mt 7:21). Prayer is not merely a matter of verbalizing our faith and love. It is also a matter of living this personal relationship which we proclaim in word. In this sense we can understand what it means to pray always.

The problem of not having enough time to pray can be partially solved by recognizing that one's whole life with all its responsibilities and human relationships can become a meaningful expression of one's response to Christ. This kind of genuine prayer will dispose one for more formal periods of prayer.

Yet, seeing one's life as prayer should not become an excuse for omitting the practice of taking time out from one's ordinary tasks in order to relate in conscious dialogue with God. That these two aspects of prayer are intimately connected can be seen from an analogy with human relationship. In a happy marriage husband and wife live their lives for one another. All they do becomes a sign of their love relationship. Even when separated they are orientated toward each other. However, in order for this to be, there must be times when they communicate in a deeply personal way. To the extent that they fail to do this, their lives will drift apart.

Our relationship with Christ is similar to this. It is by spending time listening and speaking to Christ in prayer that the rest of our lives can become more consciously directed to Him.

Prayer through Christ

In Old Testament times God spoke to His people in a variety of ways. In the fullness of time He has spoken to us through His Son (Heb 1:1, 2). Jesus is the Word of God made flesh (Jn 1:14). It is He alone who has made the Father known to us (Jn 1:18). No one can go to the Father except through Christ (Jn 14:6).

Christian prayer involves listening to God the Father speak to us through Jesus Christ. It must be based, therefore, on a personal knowledge of Christ who now communicates to us through the Scriptures and the sacraments, as well as other ways. Prayer for the Christian is personal response to Christ that leads us to respond with Him to His Father.

Christ, then, is at the very center of a Christian's prayer.

Essential Elements of Prayer

Too often there has been a tendency to identify prayer with certain forms of prayer, and to put more stress on the length of our prayers than on their quality. Perhaps one of the main reasons for this was that grace has been frequently looked upon as a quantitative thing that grew according to the number of prayers one recited.

The New Testament serves as a corrective here. The life of grace consists in knowing the one true God and Jesus Christ whom He sends (Jn 17:3). Growth in this life cannot be measured in terms of quantity, but only in terms of personal union and friendship (cf. Jn 15:14, 15; 17:21). Accordingly, in speaking of prayer, Christ emphasizes the interior disposition of the heart, and warns against ostentation and verbosity (Mt 6:5-7).

Prayer is meant to deepen our friendship with God. Accordingly, an analogy with human friendship will be helpful in understanding a proper approach to prayer. In order for the friendship between two people to grow there must be personal communication between them. The sincerity and spontaneity of their communication is far more important than the frequency of their encounters. In each case the two persons involved must determine which ways of expressing friendship will intensify their relationship. What works in one situation may be counter-productive in another.

Our prayer life bears a similarity to this. In order for friendship with Christ to deepen there must be personal communication in prayer. However, the details regarding the time, place and length of our prayer, and the particular types of prayer one utilizes cannot be ends in themselves. They must serve the purpose of prayer, namely, growth in one's personal union with Christ.

Simplification of Prayer

When two people do not know each other very well, they often find themselves trying quite hard to keep the conversation going. The weather, the game, last night's TV show are all brought up to prevent a conversation lag. When silence does ensue, the situation becomes awkward and uncomfortable. As they come to know each other better they share more deeply their thoughts and feelings. They even come to the point where they are comfortable in silence together. Indeed, their very silence becomes a sharing.

In prayer there is a similar kind of growth that takes place. In the earlier stages of one's prayer life a great effort is made to fill the time with wordy formulas. There is often a reliance on lengthy formulas of the prayer-book variety, or on the repetition of memorized prayers. Unless the words keep coming, there is fear that one is not praying.

As the ability to pray grows, there is often experienced a dissatisfaction with earlier forms that at one time had been helpful. Formularized prayers tend to give way to spontaneous dialogue. Words become less important, and gradually these yield to periods of silent awareness of the presence of Christ.

When one experiences this happening, the tendency may be to interpret the distaste for previous methods of prayer as a loss of fervor or a diminishing of faith. Hence, many strive to cling to these earlier forms of prayer even after they have served their usefulness. However, if the analogy with human friendship is borne in mind, then it should come as no surprise that, as union with Christ grows, prayer tends to become more simplified. One should then be willing to put aside those types of prayer that are no longer helpful, in order to grow in genuine prayer.

Shared Prayer

A Christian is not called to live his life of faith in isolation, but as a member of a community. The only way a community of persons is formed is by personal communication. The Christian community grows through a mutual sharing of that which makes the members Christian, namely, their faith and love of Christ. One of the important ways of doing this is through a sharing of our prayer life.

This kind of sharing takes place in liturgical celebrations. There are also nonliturgical ways in which a family, a community of religious, or other groups of Christians come together to pray. It is the latter type of shared prayer that we speak of here.

In considering this type of prayer, a distinction must be made between merely reciting prayers together, and really sharing one's prayer life with others. While the group recitation of form prayers (divine office, rosary, etc.) can be one way of sharing prayer, it is quite possible for people to recite prayers with one another without communicating to each other anything of their personal understanding of faith in and love for Christ. This latter is often better achieved by a group through spontaneous prayer, through the reading of the Scriptures, followed by the expression of personal reflections, and through periods of silent meditation.

This kind of approach to group prayer will contribute a great deal to deepening the understanding and love that is productive of unity within a family, a religious community, or a parish. It is also an excellent way to help the very young develop a genuine prayer life.

CONCLUSION

As Christians we can learn much from the manner in which Christ himself prayed. Chapter 17 of St. John's Gospel is known as the priestly prayer of Christ:

> Father, the hour has come:
> glorify your Son
> so that your Son may glorify you;
> and, through the power over all mankind
>   that you have given him,
> let him give eternal life to all those you have
>   entrusted to him.

And eternal life is this:
to know you,
the only true God,
and Jesus Christ whom you have sent.

I have glorified you on earth
and finished the work
that you gave me to do.
Now, Father, it is time for you to glorify me
with that glory I had with you
before ever the world was.

I have made your name known
to the men you took from the world to give me.
They were yours and you gave them to me,
and they have kept your word.

Now at last they know
that all you have given me
    comes indeed from you;
for I have given them
the teaching you gave to me,
and they have truly accepted this,
    that I came from you,
and have believed that it was you who sent me.

I pray for them;
I am not praying for the world
but for those you have given me,
because they belong to you:
all I have is yours
and all you have is mine,
and in them I am glorified.

I am not in the world any longer,
but they are in the world,
and I am coming to you.

Holy Father,
keep those you have given me true to your name,
so that they may be one like us.

While I was with them,
I kept those you had given me true to your name.
I have watched over them and not one is lost
except the one who chose to be lost,
and this was to fulfill the scriptures.

But now I am coming to you
and while still in the world I say these things
to share my joy with them to the full.

I passed your word on to them,
and the world hated them,
because they belong to the world
no more than I belong to the world.
I am not asking you to remove them
    from the world,
but to protect them from the evil one.
They do not belong to the world
any more than I belong to the world.

Consecrate them in the truth;
your word is truth.
As you sent me into the world,
I have sent them into the world,
and for their sake I consecrate myself
so that they too may be consecrated in truth.

I pray not only for these,
but for those also
who through their words will believe in me.
May they all be one.

Father, may they be one in us,
as you are in me and I am in you,
so that the world may believe it was you
    who sent me.

I have given them the glory you gave to me,
that they may be one as we are one.
With me in them and you in me,
may they be so completely one
that the world will realize that it was you
    who sent me
and that I have loved them
    as much as you loved me.

Father,
I want those you have given me
to be with me where I am,
so that they may always see the glory
you have given me
because you loved me
before the foundation of the world.

Father, Righteous One,
the world has not known you,
but I have known you,
and these have known
that you have sent me.
I have made your name known to them
and will continue to make it known,
so that the love with which you loved me
    may be in them,
and so that I may be in them.

Chapter Two

PRAYER OF

PETITION

PRAYER OF PETITION

The preceding chapter dealt with prayer in general. Here we will consider specifically that type of prayer which we call petition.

There are two extremes to be avoided in regard to this kind of prayer. First, there are those who identify all prayer with petition. Some of the people in this group pray only when they find themselves in distress and in need of help. Others pray regularly, but their prayers have become an endless stream of asking God to give them this or that. In this framework God is seen as an everlasting Santa Claus always ready to fulfill the whims of his small children. This type of praying often blinds us to our own personal responsibilities. Indeed, if things don't turn out the way we desire, we can put the blame on God.

The other extreme may well be a reaction to this kind of mentality. It consists in ridiculing any form of petition to God. Some would see such petition as self-centered. Others reject it as needless, saying that God already knows what is going to happen anyway, and "how can we change that?" Still others look upon this form of prayer as an immature running to "daddy" for those things we should be working out ourselves. The main problem with this extreme is that it finds itself in direct conflict with the clear directive of Christ often repeated in the New Testament: to ask for anything at all in His name (e.g. Jn 14:13, 14; 15:7).

In this consideration of prayer of petition we would like to show:

a) that prayer of petition also involves worship and thanksgiving;

b) that it implies a commitment to explore the possible, and to accept the Father's will;

c) that the promise that we will receive what we ask for in Christ's name must be understood in a proper way.

PRAYER OF PETITION INVOLVES WORSHIP AND THANKSGIVING

While there is validity in classifying prayer according to types such as worship, thanksgiving, and petition, it is important to realize that there is an overlapping. Prayer of petition cannot be adequately understood unless we appreciate the fact that turning to God in petition is itself a form of worship.

To adore or worship God is to acknowledge Him as the author of life, and the one upon whom we ultimately depend for our existence and our well-being. Petition involves this realization. Cognizant of our limitations, we turn to God as the source of strength. Aware of our darkness we acknowledge Him as one who can give us light. Imprisoned by our failure to love, we go to Him who is love, that we may be transformed by love.

Petition also implies gratitude. If one values what he has received he will utilize it to the fullest. If he appreciates and respects what the giver has to give, he will be open to receive more.

We ask God for an increase of His gifts because of the value we see in them. We show our gratitude to God for all He has done for us by being receptive to His further giving. We give clear sign of this receptivity by asking God to satisfy our needs.

PRAYER OF PETITION IMPLIES A COMMITMENT TO EXPLORE THE POSSIBLE, AND TO ACCEPT THE FATHER'S WILL

Christ gives an excellent example of prayer of petition in His anguish in the garden the night before He died. " 'Abba (Father)!' he said, 'everything is possible for you. Take this cup away from me. But let it be as you, not I, would have it' " (Mk 14:36). Christ acknowledges that all things are possible to the Father, and in His prayer He explores the possibility that the cup be taken away. He had been face to face with attempts on His life before, and had passed from the danger. When His enemies tried to throw Him down the cliff at Nazareth, He slipped through the crowd and walked away (Lk 4:30). When they picked up stones to throw at Him, He hid himself and left the temple (Jn 8:59). Now, on the very night He is to be taken prisoner He asks, "If it is possible, let this cup pass me by" (Mt 26:39).

But His prayer continues: "If this cup cannot pass me by without my drinking it, your will be done!" (Mt 26:42) Everything is possible to the Father, but not everything is of equal value for the growth of the individual, and the well-being of mankind. The Father's will is the glorification of Christ, and the salvation of all mankind (cf Jn 17:1-5; 10:17-18; Heb 10:9). Accordingly, Christ prays that His Father's will be done. He is open to the possibility that the only way the cup can pass by is that He drink it. His prayer of petition becomes an expression of His acceptance of His Father's will, even to the drinking of the cup. In the spirit of this prayer Christ does accept His death knowing that His Father will not abandon Him (Lk 23:46), and that His hour of death is really His hour of glory (Jn 12:23-28; Lk 24:26).

Christ bids us to present our petitions to the Father in His name (Jn 14:13-14; 15:16; 16:23-24). That means we are to pray in the spirit of Christ. Our prayer of petition must involve for us what it did for Christ, an exploration of the possible, and openness to the Father's will.

Exploration of the Possible:

To pray to God for help is to recognize the fact that there are many things not possible to us without His aid. To pray for His help is already an effort on our part to explore this realm of possibility. We pray that God does for us what is possible. We pray that He gives us the help we need to do all in our power to explore and discover whatever solutions are possible.

Understood in this sense, prayer of petition can never be an excuse for washing our hands of human responsibility, and leaving it all up to God. We must pray with a humble awareness of our own limitations, and with real belief in God's strengthening power. However, it is important to realize that His power does not magically take over for us.[1] Rather He gives us His light and strength to come to grips with the reality of our situation, to explore the possibilities that are already at hand, and to pioneer beyond the borders of our present limitations.

In light of this an inadequacy can be seen in the distinction made in the oft-repeated quote that tells us to pray as if everything depended on God and to work as if everything depended on ourselves. It would seem more accurate to say that we must pray as if everything depends both on God and on ourselves, and we must work as if everything depends on God and on ourselves. This is the reality. Hence both our prayer and our work should reflect it.

While we should pray realizing that we can do nothing without God, our prayer should also reflect the awareness that, in order for God to accomplish in

---

[1]Indeed, God can go beyond our limitations, and miracles can happen. But these can never be presumed. While we can be aware of the possibility of a miracle, our prayer must reflect first of all a willingness on our part to do all that lies within our power with God's help.

us what He wishes, our cooperation is required. Prayer of petition, then, is not only a manifestation of our total dependence on God, it is also a personal commitment to face up to our responsibility and do our share. This kind of prayer then becomes a force moving us to work with a humble openness to God's directing light and power, and with resolute dedication to operate to the fullness of our powers.

This aspect of prayer of petition can be illustrated by any number of concrete examples.[2] For our purpose here we will consider three of the petitions that people commonly pray for: a good job, protection from crime, safe travel. All of these are valid objects of our prayer, but all must involve a facing up to personal responsibility.

Good job: Obviously jobs don't drop down from the sky. Prayer in this regard is not for magic intervention, but for help that we might have the strength to work harder to become better qualified and to search in the right places. We pray that we will meet the right opportunity at the right moment.

---

[2]The personal responsibility involved in prayer of petition will be reflected throughout our consideration of the petitions of the Lord's Prayer in chapter four.

We commit ourselves to the task of creating an atmosphere that will enable as many as possible to work according to their qualifications.

Protection from crime: Prayer for this must include the willingness to take the ordinary means to protect oneself and to avoid the obvious dangers. It must also be a prayer for ourselves that we be moved out of our apathy to do what is possible to change those conditions that breed crime: ghettos, outmoded prison conditions, and social oppression.

Safe travel: We should pray that we have the attention and concern to operate vehicles intelligently and with care, and to avoid the obstacles to safety such as sleepiness, drinking, and improper equipment. If we are serious about this prayer we must be willing to support the continued research and work required to keep improving safe means and conditions of travel. We must manifest concern for the needs of those responsible for the safety of travelers.

These examples illustrate what is true of all prayer of petition. It can never be an escape from reality. Approached in the proper spirit it is a sign of our desire to be helped by God to face the realities and responsibilities of our life. It is a manifestation of our intent to do all in our power to explore the possible.

Openness to the Father's Will:

Genuine prayer of petition possesses another important component, that is, a surrender in faith and trust to the loving will of the Father. This implies that we have already sought His will in doing all we can to help ourselves.[3] Having explored what is possible, we face realities that are beyond our control. Some of these are due to the liabilities of the present human condition: ignorance, sin, error, and helplessness in the face of certain forces of nature that are greater than we are. Others are due to the fact that part of the mystery of life is that loss, pain, and suffering are the price for growth in life, love, and joy. The ultimate inevitability is, of course, death. While it can be postponed, eventually death to mortal life is the only way of entrance into immortal life.

To ask for something in the name of Christ is to pray, believing that the

---

[3]The will of God is difficult to treat. We constantly have the tendency to blame God's will for those things which result from man's lack of imagination and effort.

Father wills not death but life, not destruction but restoration. It is to pray with the realization that if the cup cannot pass away without our drinking it, the Father will give us the strength to drink it not to our loss, but to our salvation. If, once we have done our part, we accept the inevitable as an expression of the Father's love, we can face the reality without being choked by self-pity and bitterness. With His help we can grow through the experience to deeper faith and love, and to greater personhood.

ASK IN CHRIST'S NAME
AND YOU WILL RECEIVE

Christ prayed the night before He died that, if possible, the cup be taken away. The Father did not remove the cup; but He heard the prayer of Christ. In the words of the evangelist, "an angel appeared to him, coming from heaven to give him strength" (Lk 22:43). This gives us a key to understanding the meaning of Christ's promise: "Ask, and it will be given you; search, and you will find; knock, and the door will be opened to you. For the one who asks always receives; the one who searches always finds; the one who knocks will always have the door opened to him" (Mt 7:7-8).

There are several inadequacies in the way these words are commonly understood. First, many forget that Christ is speaking about prayer in His name. That is an important qualification that has many implications, as we have tried to show in the preceding sections of this chapter. Secondly, many interpret these words in a simplistic way, as if praying for something was like putting a coin in a vending machine.

In the previous chapter we noted that prayer is not our effort to get God concerned about us. He is already aware and concerned about what we need (Mt 6:8). We pray to Him so that we might grow in awareness of His love. We respond to Him, for He is already communicating to us. The very fact that we are able to pray is already a sign that He is doing something for us in our situation. By exposing ourselves to Him we find light and strength, whatever the eventuality be.

The one who asks in Christ's name always receives. In fact, he has already begun to receive before he asks; otherwise he could not even ask. To the one who knocks, the door will be opened. For Christ is already at the door knocking for us to open so that we may share with Him (Rv 3:19, 20). The one who searches will find, since Christ himself is the one who has come to seek out and save what was lost (Lk 19:10).

CONCLUSION

Prayer of petition, adequately understood, is not an egoistic centering on oneself. It is a turning to God with realistic awareness of one's own condition, and with belief in His abiding love. It is a commitment to improve what can be changed, and to accept in a creative way what is beyond human control.

Chapter Three

PRAYER OF A

SUFFERING MAN

A Reflection on
Psalm Twenty-two

PRAYER OF
A SUFFERING MAN

From earliest times man has been disturbed and puzzled by the mystery of suffering. Confronted with tragedy, believing man has ever been tempted to question why God has forsaken him, and allowed evil to beset him. In Psalm 22, the psalmist, encountering persecution, cries out with personal anguish, "My God, my God, why have you deserted me?" What is significant is the fact that the same author goes on to answer his own question. God has not, and will not forsake him. Accordingly, the psalm ends with a hymn of praise, and in a spirit of hope and victory.

This psalm takes on added significance for the Christian, since it is the prayer Christ begins to pray as He dies at the hands of His enemies (Mt 27:46). To aid in the reflection that follows, we will first present the psalm in its entirety.

1   My God, my God, why have you deserted me?
    How far from saving me, the words I groan!
2   I call all day, my God, but you never answer,
    all night long I call and cannot rest.

3   Yet, Holy One, you
     who make your home in the praises of Israel,
4   in you our fathers put their trust,
     they trusted and you rescued them;
5   they called to you for help and they were saved,
     they never trusted you in vain.

6   Yet here am I, now more worm than man,
     scorn of mankind, jest of the people,
7   all who see me jeer at me,
     they toss their heads and sneer,
8   'He relied on Yahweh, let Yahweh save him!
     If Yahweh is his friend, let Him rescue him!'

9   Yet you drew me out of the womb,
     you entrusted me to my mother's breasts;
10   placed on your lap from my birth,
     from my mother's womb
        you have been my God.
11   Do not stand aside: trouble is near,
     I have no one to help me!

12   A herd of bulls surrounds me,
     strong bulls of Bashan close in on me;
13   their jaws are agape for me,
     like lions tearing and roaring.

14   I am like water draining away,
     my bones are all disjointed,
     my heart is like wax,
     melting inside me;
15   my palate is drier than a potsherd
     and my tongue is stuck to my jaw.

16　A pack of dogs surrounds me,
　　a gang of villains closes me in;
　　they tie me hand and foot
　　and leave me lying in the dust of death.

17　I can count every one of my bones,
　　and there they glare at me, gloating;
18　they divide my garments among them
　　and cast lots for my clothes.

19　Do not stand aside, Yahweh.
　　O my strength, come quickly to my help;
20　rescue my soul from the sword,
　　my dear life from the paw of the dog,
21　save me from the lion's mouth,
　　my poor soul from the wild bulls' horns!

22　Then I shall proclaim your name to my brothers,
　　praise you in full assembly:
23　you who fear Yahweh, praise him!
　　Entire race of Jacob, glorify him!
　　Entire race of Israel, revere him!

24　For he has not despised
　　or disdained the poor man in his poverty,
　　has not hidden his face from him,
　　but has answered him when he called.

25　You are the theme of my praise
　　　in the Great Assembly,
　　I perform my vows in the presence of those
　　　who fear him.

26　The poor will receive

as much as they want to eat.
Those who seek Yahweh will praise him.
Long life to their hearts!

27 The whole earth, from end to end, will re-
          member and come back to Yahweh;
     All the families of the nations
          will bow down before him.
28 For Yahweh reigns, the ruler of nations!
29 Before him all the prosperous of the earth
          will bow down,
     before him will bow
          all who go down to the dust.
30 And my soul will live for him,
          my children will serve him;
31 men will proclaim the Lord
          to generations still to come,
     his righteousness to a people yet unborn.
          All this he has done.

THE PSALM ITSELF

The psalmist begins by verbalizing the aloneness he experiences in his plight. He has prayed to God day and night, but his words seem useless. To all appearances God is distant. No answer is heard. Rest is impossible (vv. 1-2).

The author reflects further. He recalls that this same God, who now seems to be so far away, is the Holy One, who makes His home in the praises of Israel. He is the God in whom the Israelite ancestors put their trust. They were rescued and saved. They never trusted in vain (vv. 3-5).

That consoling thought already reflects hope. However, it does not wipe away the cruel realities of his present affliction. Here he is, seeming more like a worm than a man, scorned and jeered at. There is no one to offer help: He relied on Yahweh, let Yahweh save him! (vv. 6-8)

Again, the psalmist steps back from his preoccupation with his suffering, and places his situation in the context of his experience of God's concern and love for him during his own lifetime. The Lord of Israel is the One who drew him out of the womb and entrusted him to his mother's breasts. From his birth he has been the recipient of God's tender love (vv. 9-10). In light of these considerations, the author is moved to turn again to God for help. "Do not stand aside: trouble is near" (v. 11).

The depth and persistence of the author's anguish is evidenced in the next four stanzas (vv. 12-18). Through a series of vivid metaphors he provides the reader with an insight into the acuteness of his suffering. A herd of bulls is closing in on him. They are like lions ready to devour him. He is like water draining away. His bones are disjointed, his heart is like wax, and his mouth is completely dry. A gang of villains tie his hands and feet. Leaving him to die, they turn their attention to his clothes. They divide his garments among them.

Having described his plight, the psalmist centers the remainder of his prayer on Yahweh. With deepening trust he begs God to rescue him from the paw of the dog, and the mouth of the lion (vv. 19-21). With victory already in sight, the author offers his thanks to God (vv. 22-31). He shall praise Him in full assembly, for the Lord has not despised the poor man in his poverty, but has answered him. The poor will receive as much as they want to eat. Those who seek Yahweh will praise Him. The whole earth will remember and come back to Him. Men will proclaim the Lord to generations yet to come. All this the Lord has done.

CHRIST AND PSALM 22

Those familiar with what have been known as the "Seven Last Words" spoken by Christ on the cross recognize, "My God, my God, why hast thou forsaken me?" as the fifth of these words. Unfortunately, much of the popular treatment of this statement of Christ has failed to reflect its Old Testament background. As a consequence much attention has been directed to the false question of how Christ could fall into despair, and doubt His Father's love. Once we realize that Christ, in accord with His Jewish heritage, is praying the opening words of Psalm 22, it is clear that there is no question of despair here. Christ chooses as His dying prayer the psalm in which a man suffering persecution answers his opening question with grateful trust in God, and with keen hope of victory.

In the Gospels, Christ gives clear evidence of His awareness of the rejection and persecution that are the lot of the prophet (Mt 23:33-37; Lk 4:24). He speaks of His own death (Lk 9:22, 44), and warns His apostles that they too will suffer for His name (Mt 10:17-25). However, He sees this reality not as a form of self-destruction, but as having redemptive value. He speaks of His own death as His hour of glory (Jn 12:23). It is like a grain of wheat falling into the earth and dying, in order to yield a rich harvest (Jn 12:24).

Christ's choice of Psalm 22 for His prayer is fitting for two reasons. First, there is a similarity between the plight of the psalmist and the suffering of Jesus.

This is brought out by the fact that the evangelist describes many aspects of Christ's Passion in language taken from Psalm 22. (See, for example, Mt 27:35, 39, 43; Lk 23:34). Secondly, the closing stanzas of the psalm parallel the positive attitude of Christ in facing death. The psalmist concludes his prayer by proclaiming his trust that God will save him, and that all mankind will turn to Yahweh. Christ dies entrusting His Spirit to the Father (Lk 23:46), and aware that if He be raised up He will draw all things to himself (Jn 12:32).

OUR PRAYER
IN TIME OF SUFFERING

When faced with sorrow, the average person is usually tempted to question God in terms similar to the opening words of the 22nd psalm. "If there is a God, how could there be so much evil in the world?" "If God is good, how could He let this happen to me?" When tragedy strikes, our tendency is to center our attention on the evil, and then to proceed to question the existence, wisdom, or love of God.

Psalm 22 teaches an important lesson. The psalmist reflects on God's goodness, and then is able to see his suffering in the perspective of God's love. The Christian has all the more reason to be able to do this. God has manifested His love through all the gifts of life He has given us. The most visible expression of His love has been the death and Resurrection of Jesus Christ. "A man can have no greater love than to lay down his life for his friends" (Jn 15:13).

An essential part of Christian faith must be a deep conviction that God is love, and is concerned about every aspect of man's well-being. This awareness of the love of the Father and of Christ must be our starting point. Then our troubles and sorrows can be seen in the context of this love. Hardship should not occasion our seriously doubting God's love; we should be able to say with St. Paul that nothing can separate us from the love of Christ.

Chapter Four

THE LORD'S

OWN PRAYER

THE LORD'S OWN PRAYER

St. Matthew in his Gospel records our Lord's own prayer in chapter six, verses nine through thirteen.

Our Father in heaven,
may your name be held holy,
your kingdom come,
your will be done,
on earth as in heaven.
Give us today our daily bread.
And forgive us our debts,
as we have forgiven
    those who are in debt to us.
And do not put us to the test,
but save us from the evil one.

INSIGHTS AND IMPLICATIONS

Christ has given us the clearest indication of His prayer life, and of what ours should be, by that prayer which has come to be known as His own.

In this chapter we will reflect on each of the phrases of this prayer. This reflection will serve a twofold purpose: it will give us some insight into the prayer life of Christ, and it will bring into focus some implications this has for our own life of prayer.

Our Father

Christ addresses God as Father. He does not speak to Him in the abstract language of the philosophers: the infinite supreme being, pure act, unmoved mover, and "almighty and everlasting God." Neither does Christ address Him merely in the categories of the Old Testament: the God of Abraham, of Moses, of Isaac; the God of the Old Covenant. He speaks to Him in a way that no man before ever could. He begins His prayer with the word "Father," a word that immediately suggests the unique personal relationship that exists between them; a word that sums up the new revelation which Christ came to proclaim.

God is His Father, and Christ can pray "Father," because He acknowledges and accepts the reality that all He has He receives from the Father. He can pray "Father," because He accepts what it means to be Son, and is willing to live out to the fullest His filial response to the Father, with all that implies, even unto death and Resurrection. To call His Father "Father" is to call himself "Son," and hence reaffirm His response to this relationship.

Jesus goes further. He calls His Father *"Our* Father." His prayer not only highlights His personal relationship with the Father, it emphasizes the relationship He has with His fellow-man. Because Christ loves the Father, He comes to do the will of His Father. He makes us sons and daughters.

In addressing His Father as *Our* Father, Christ declares His identity with our humanity. He manifests His acceptance of all mankind without exception and without qualification. He implies what His redemptive work is about. He gives us the gift of the Spirit, so that with Him we may cry out, "Abba, Father" (Gal 4:4-6).

This is the prayer that Christ invites us, indeed challenges us, to say. Dare we say it? Too often we don't. We much rather address God in philosophical terms and emphasize His might, His eternity, and His supremacy. Such titles have meaning, but they do not bring into focus the essential dimension of Christian revelation that God is Father and Jesus is His Son. Nor do they sufficiently challenge us to the filial response Christ demands.

To say, "almighty and everlasting God," immediately brings into consciousness those aspects of God that distance Him from us. He is all-powerful, I am fragile. He is eternal, I am mortal.

He is Lord, I am subject. It is more convenient to pray in these terms, because the response demanded in this kind of relationship is less exacting. The omnipotent Being is satisfied by the subservience of His creature.

To call God "Father" is to focus our attention on the essential relationship that only Christ can make possible for us. It means that we accept Christ as Son, and that we proclaim the Father of Jesus Christ as our Father. To say "Father" is to accept our own identity as His sons and daughters, and hence to commit ourselves to live this relationship. The demands of filial response cannot be neatly packaged or manipulated. They are unlimited.

Christ does not have us pray in isolation. Rather, He bids us to pray in union with our fellow-man. The Father of Jesus Christ is not just my Father, He is *our* Father, the One who gives life and love and concern to all mankind. To call God "Father," and mean it, is to say "brother, sister" to *every* man and woman. To say "Father" honestly means that we strive to live as brothers and sisters with one another. It means that we are willing to create for others an atmosphere of understanding, love and concern that will enrich their lives, whether this be in the context of our home, our place of work, our neighborhood, or the world.

May your name be held holy

For the Hebrew, the name of a person meant the person. Hence, to pray "may your name be held holy" is to pray that the Father be regarded holy by mankind. This implies that we are committing ourselves to get to know Him as the source of holiness, so that experiencing Him as the One who alone is holy, we ourselves may become holy. We thus become the visible signs through whom others can come to know God as holy.

In the Gospel, Christ makes clear that love is the ultimate norm of Christian holiness. John, in his first Epistle, indicates this when he says that "God is love" (1 Jn 4:8), and "to live a holy life is to be holy just as he is holy" (1 Jn 3:7). God's name is held holy when we believe in His love, and through the reflection of His love in our lives, enable others to experience His love.

Your kingdom come

Christ prays to the Father that His kingdom come. This prayer is said with the realization that His mission is to proclaim and visibly manifest that the kingdom of God is already here. Christ himself is the sign of His Father's abiding presence among men. When Christ prays "your kingdom come," He signifies His acceptance of the work His Father has given Him, namely, to establish now His kingdom among men, a task that is only brought to fulfillment at the end of time. Christ's prayer that the kingdom come is not just verbal. It is lived by Him in the reality of His total dedication to go about and plant the seeds of the kingdom in the hearts of men.

The kind of kingdom that Jesus is talking about can only be understood in the light of the entire Gospel. He makes clear that His kingdom is not of the same type as the kingdoms of this world (Jn 17:36). He corrects some of the false concepts which many Jews at the time had of the kind of Messiah He would be. He has not come to establish a material utopia. Accordingly, He refuses to change stones into loaves of bread (Mt 4:3-4), and He flees from the crowd when they want to make Him their king after He has performed the miracle of the multiplication of loaves (Jn 6:15). He did not intend to build a political and financial empire. Thus He refuses to accept the power and glory of the kingdoms of the world which are offered to Him if He but worship the evil one (Lk 4:5-8). Finally, His kingdom is not of the type that is to be secured by means of physical violence. Hence He refuses to allow His disciples to protect Him with arms (Jn 18:11, 36).

His kingdom is a kingdom founded on truth, freedom, and loving service. This is why He came into the world, to communicate the truth, so that the truth would make men free (Jn 18:37; 8:32). He comes to be a light to all in the world, so that those who are open to the light might receive the power to be sons and daughters of God (Jn 1:9, 12). His kingdom is not one in which those in authority lord it over others. Rather, His kingdom is one in which those in positions of responsibility fulfill their role by feeding and serving others (Lk 22:24-27; Jn 13:13-16; 21:15-17).

Christ prays that the Father's kingdom, already manifest through Him, may increasingly influence our lives until it comes to fulfillment. This prayer Christ seals by His own life and death, and by His taking up of life again.

It is this prayer that Christ bids us to pray. If we pray this way, we must be willing to cooperate in the task of building and advancing this type of kingdom in our midst. While the kingdom does not come to fulfillment until the end of time, it is meant to be lived and experienced right now. The specific mission of the Christian community is to proclaim that the kingdom of Christ is already in our midst, and to work so that this kingdom may be ever more reflected in the experience of mankind.

The kingdom of God which we pray for, and which we are called to advance, cannot be of the type of this world. It is not to be a political stronghold, nor a financial empire. Neither is it characterized by privilege and dominance. Rather, His kingdom is constituted by people whose lives are affected by the saving action of Jesus Christ. The unique characteristics of the kingdom which Christ advances are aptly described in the preface for the Mass of Christ the King: it is

> an eternal and universal kingdom;
> a kingdom of truth and life,
> a kingdom of holiness and grace,
> a kingdom of justice, love and peace.

When, in the Lord's Prayer we pray "your kingdom come," we are really praying that something happens to us so that mankind may become the type of community the Father wishes. We pray that we become personally transformed so that all our relationships echo the love of Christ. By this prayer we manifest our serious intent to be about the work of bringing our relationships into line with God's kind of kingdom. To see the implications of this, let us consider some of the characteristics of the kingdom highlighted in the preface just cited.

A universal kingdom: This kingdom does not impose on all its members one cultural expression of faith, life-style, and worship. It is not a clique, nor composed merely of the elite. Rather it is open to all people regardless of race, nationality, and socioeconomic class. To pray for this *universal* kingdom to come is to commit ourselves to the task of rooting out of our midst all types of prejudice, and to respect the fact that the one life in Christ can have many valid cultural expressions.

A kingdom of truth: A kingdom of truth involves much more than the absence of error and deceit. It is built on an honest acceptance of reality and the mutual communication of truth. A prayer that this kind of kingdom be advanced suggests our willingness to be open to the fullness of truth which God continues to reveal through Jesus Christ. In addition, it suggests our renewed commitment to live and spread this good news. This means that we will not be afraid of the truth, and that we are willing to explore all the avenues to clearer and deeper knowledge about the world, about ourselves, and about the meaning of our relationship with God.

A kingdom of life: To build a kingdom of truth is, indeed, to build a kingdom of life. Christ himself defines eternal life: "Eternal life is this: to know you, the only true God, and Jesus Christ whom you have sent" (Jn 17:3).

A kingdom of holiness and grace: This kind of kingdom is one in which people are aware of the abiding presence of Father, Son and Spirit, and reflect this awareness and love in their lives, in their attitudes and in their dealings with others.

A kingdom of justice and love: This is a reality when all persons are recognized as endowed with a basic equality and human dignity. This aspect of the kingdom is achieved only to the extent that we are willing to give each individual his due, and to love our neighbor as ourselves.

A kingdom of peace: Peace is not something which is merely received, or just kept. It is something which must ever be created anew. Perhaps that is why Christ does not say blessed are the peace-keepers, but rather blessed are the peace-makers (Mt 5:9). If we are serious about praying for a kingdom of peace, we must dedicate ourselves to the task of rooting out of our lives the obstacles to peace, such as jealousies, intolerance, avarice, misunderstanding, and hatred. We must plant the seeds that are indispensable to the growth of peace: communication, understanding, patience, generosity, and love.

This phrase of the Lord's Prayer, "your kingdom come," is not, then, an expression of mere desire that God do something at the end of time, even despite us. It expresses our desire that His kingdom be already reflected in our lives now, on this earth, even though in an incomplete way. This means that we are willing to do our part, all in preparation for that time when His kingdom will come to us in its fullness forever.

Your Will Be Done On Earth As In Heaven

Christ prays that the will of His Father be fulfilled here on earth as it is in heaven. Elsewhere Christ made clear that the two greatest commandments upon which the whole Law and Prophets depend are to love the Lord with one's whole heart, soul, and mind, and to love one's neighbor as oneself (Mt 22:34-40). The doing of God's will is nothing less than striving to be perfect in love as the heavenly Father is perfect (Mt 5:43-48). This is what persons in heaven have achieved. Consequently, what Christ is praying for is that we ever grow toward the fullness of love.

Christ, of course, reflects this prayer in His life. He fulfills His Father's will even unto death (Jn 10:17, 18; Philip 2:6-11). He could show no greater love than to lay down His life for His fellow-man (Jn 15:12, 13).

If we sincerely pray this part of the Lord's Prayer, we are really asking for God's help that we grow in our ability to fulfill His will perfectly. In other words, we are reaffirming our desire and intent to become more like Christ, and grow in love of the Father and in love of all people.

Give Us Today Our Daily Bread

This part of the prayer manifests another aspect of Christ's concern for the needs of man. His Father is the author of life, and the one who sustains it and enables it to grow. With profound awareness of His Father's abiding love for man, Jesus prays that we receive our daily bread.

Christ's life bears out the fact that He realizes that while His Father is the source of all good, these gifts do not come in a vacuum, but through the cooperative work and sharing of human beings. His prayer, "give us today our daily bread," is not intended to absolve man of His responsibility to work for His bread. Rather, Christ leads the way and shows how man must be the instrument through whom God's bread is given. After He raises the daughter of Jairus from the dead, He shows concern for this basic physical need and "told them to give her something to eat" (Lk 8:55). When the 4,000 had been with Him for three days in a deserted place, He would not send them off hungry lest they collapse on the way. Accordingly, He gave them bread and fish in abundance and they all ate as much as they wanted (Mt 15:32-39). After the Resurrection He is seen preparing breakfast for some of His disciples on the shore of the Sea of Tiberias (Jn 21:9-14). Finally, He makes clear that for us to be His followers and enter into His kingdom we must be sensitive to all the needs of others; we must feed the hungry, for what we do to them we do to Christ (Mt 25:31-46).

Christ not only reflects His prayer of concern for daily bread by giving bread to others. He actually becomes for us the bread of life. In the sixth chapter of John's Gospel, Christ's feeding of the 5,000 through the multiplication of the loaves is presented as a sign that He himself is our bread of life. He is our bread, for He is the Son come down from heaven, and anyone who sees and believes in Him shall have eternal life (Jn 6:32-40). He has become our bread, for now risen, Christ gives us the gift of himself in Eucharist. Anyone who eats His flesh and drinks His blood shall have life forever, and will be raised up on the last day (Jn 6:53, ff.).

All of this teaches us how to pray this request. This prayer must be an expression of our concern that everyone receive his share of bread today. To pray this sincerely means that we are willing to do all in our power to see that God's gift of bread be a daily living reality in the lives of others. It means that we ourselves are willing to become part of the answer to this prayer.

We live this prayer each time we give to another the gift of bread, whether this be the bread of physical sustenance, the bread of wisdom, or the bread of the gift of ourselves. But the prayer must challenge us to work harder that all receive daily their bread. It must make us uncomfortable about the fact that each day over ten million Americans alone go to bed hungry, and that in some cities less than two dollars a day is spent per capita on those who reside in our prisons.[1] If we are sincere about this prayer, we must strive to explore the natural resources that have already been given us, and through advances in scientific knowledge and technology do all in our power to solve the problem of hunger in our nation and in the world.

Forgive Us Our Debts, As We Have Forgiven Those Who Are In Debt To Us

In the Gospels, Christ depicts His Father as one who loves all men, and who is always willing to forgive them their sins. The Father lets His rain fall on

---

[1] *Time,* May 17, 1971, p. 63. New Orleans Parish Prison spends $1.50 a day per prisoner.

the just and the unjust (Mt 5:45). He is the Father of the prodigal son who affectionately expresses his forgiveness and love before the son even has a chance to make his prepared speech, and who celebrates the reunion with a banquet (Lk 15:11, ff.).

Christ does not have us pray for forgiveness in order to move the Father to pardon. The Father already forgives. Since forgiveness is reconciliation, it involves a dying to sin and a turning in love to God. We pray for forgiveness as a sign of our desire to change our heart from hate to love, from darkness to light. We pray for strength and help to undergo that inner conversion without which there can be no forgiveness, and hence no reunion.

There is a connection between the Father's forgiveness of us and our forgiveness of one another. His forgiveness is made visibly manifest in our lives by our external expression of forgiveness to one another. The Father forgives by giving of himself to us in love and understanding, thus enabling us to respond to Him in a filial way. We, too, forgive others by communicating to them our understanding and love, and by creating an atmosphere that can strengthen and encourage them to respond in love.

Christ put this prayer into action. He took away sins by forgiving and healing the sinner. We live this prayer by following Christ's example.

Do Not Put Us To The Test (Lead us not into temptation)

This petition should not give the erroneous impression that God is the source of temptation. Nor does it deny the reality that the path of virtue involves a struggle with temptations and trials. What we are praying for in this request is that we have the fortitude to overcome the difficulties that can impede Christian life.

As we reflect on the human situation, it becomes evident that major obstacles which stand in the way of personal growth are man-made. It is man, for example, who has created the sub-human living conditions of the ghetto, and turned much of our prison system into a breeding place for depravity. This petition then implies concern on our part to do whatever we can to free people from those obstacles that keep them from living fully human lives.

Save Us From The Evil One

There is a tendency among humans

to blame someone other than themselves for the evil in the world. Some put the blame on God, while others point the accusing finger at the devil. While there is a transcendent power of evil from which we pray to be delivered, this portion of the Lord's Prayer should be offered with the realization that man is responsible for much of the evil in the world. Wars, oppression, and injustice are just a few examples.

This prayer should include a plea that we be delivered from the pockets of evil within ourselves that are at the root of so much of the evil that plagues mankind. We should pray that we be moved out of our apathy to do all in our power to confront evil wherever we find it, and to be instruments through whom Christ's redeeming, healing grace may be brought to bear on the ills of mankind.

CONCLUSION

In the light of these reflections, the Our Father cannot be seen as an irrelevant way of washing our hands of human responsibility and of appealing to some kind of *deus ex machina* to intervene magically. The attitudes and sentiments of the mind and heart of Christ that gave birth to this prayer led Him to total identity and involvement with humanity.

Christ now risen continues to be at the heart of human life working to bring us to share in the fulfillment which is now His (Jn 12:32). To pray this prayer in union with Him is to reflect His mind and heart. Such prayer can only lead us where it has led Him, namely to be a saving grace at the heart of human living.

EPILOGUE

One day Jesus took Peter, James, and John, and went up with them to the mountain to pray (Lk 9:28-36). This experience had an effect on each of them.

As Christ prayed, the aspect of His face was changed and His clothing became brilliant as lightning. Then Moses and Elijah appeared and spoke to Him of His passing which was to take place in Jerusalem.

On this occasion something also happened to the three disciples. They received a new insight into Christ. They saw Him in His glory. A cloud (sign of divine presence) came and covered them, and from the cloud they heard a voice saying, "This is my Son, the Chosen One. Listen to him."

Prayer is meant to have a similar effect on us. Through it we are able to grow in our personal knowledge of Christ, and become more aware of what He asks for us. For this to happen we need Christ to continue to teach us how to pray. Then, like Peter, we too may experience that "it is wonderful for us to be here" (Lk 9:33).

maturity revisited

T. L. Herlong

LIGUORI PUBLICATIONS
Liguori, Missouri 63057

FOREWORD

It has always been interesting to watch young students of the Latin language tangle with Cardinal Newman's *Apologia Pro Vita Sua.* Their ready translation leaves Newman apologizing for his life, slightly ashamed, as the boys head out for the baseball field, their murderous feat accomplished. The point is, of course, that whatever else Newman was doing, he wasn't apologizing for anything. He had become a convert to the Roman Catholic Church in a soul-searing decision, and his book was simply chapter and verse of how it was in his mind when he spent those months and years auditing the Christian ledger.

Much of the same can be said of this book. Father Herlong left the priestly ministry for two years, and returned. His pages are more interested in honesty than in apologetics and justification. It is a sort of "What happened to Joe Doe two years ago?" Herlong knows well the mother tongue and can highlight a picture with a merciless brush. He is not too happy over the general scene where some Eucharistic changes made him stagger in the late 1960's as against the shock felt by Catholics of 1910 when they were urged to very frequent

Communion. Their sacramental mentality could hardly accept that awesome approach to Divinity at the altar railing three or four times a year, and now this! So one goes on to wonder how the contemporaries of St. Jerome felt as they woke up one morning to find the world turned Arian in an excruciatingly divisive heresy. Talk about changes!

The author has his own patron saints, G.K.C., Bloy, Mauriac, etc., and when he refers to them he is hinting broadly they knew how to prelude Vatican II and would have known just as well how to activate it. Gratefully, without a doubt.

The divisions of the book into the infantilism, adolescence, and maturity of the Church make a proper podium for what is said, and yet one does come away with the idea that it is not in itself any too mature to paste labels on a pilgrim Church that is more concerned with the distant shrine than with the present condition of the road.

One thing is clear. Father Herlong is not about to stand aside and cheer as the moderns go by as if he didn't know who was leading the parade away up in front. He puts a date on the labor encyclicals just

in case that anyone has forgotten what Leo and Pius had done for the working man. I suppose what we are saying here is that there could never have been a Vatican I if there had been no Council of Trent, and there never would have been a Vatican II without a Vatican I. Without holding a crusade about it, the author makes it clear upon just whose shoulders each generation stands. Right, the one just before it. So he rather lovingly picks around at some strong names like Gerald Ellard, and in a very interesting paragraph, the true council concept of Pope John. When he has finished his say about the foibles of infantilism, the pimples of adolescence and the pleadings for maturity, he puts a strong curry comb to the council animal and gets in some fine work. If he sees doctrine confused by old wives' tales, he cuts off the tales, if such a phrase can be forgiven. He notes refreshingly that the Baltimore Catechism can still be read without danger to faith, but strongly insists that the Church is a living organism that must breathe and grow, no matter what the ecology.

To choose a sentence, "In the past few years, the official Church has shown herself reluctant to crush the creative contemporary." This is said in praise of a Church that can be as contemporary in art after

Vatican II as Leo XIII was of labor before Vatican II.

It is the same Church, and it seems that maturity is in the eyes of the beholder.

Father Herlong has a ready roof for his good substructure. He speaks of Baptism and Love in such a way that one wonders if they are two words.

Francis Lee, C.SS.R.
Assistant Editor, Liguorian Books

CONTENTS

prologue

In 1968 I retired from the active ministry. Common enough in these days. In 1970 I returned fully to the active ministry. A thing quite uncommon (perhaps because it is more difficult than retiring, as a few have experienced).

One reason for my retiring from the ministry stemmed from deep disturbance over the changing Church. Pope John opened windows which I thought should remain closed. One of the reasons for my return involved reflections from outside those opened windows. Whatever value the following words may have, they are based neither on theory nor thorough study but rather upon the personal reflections of one who has stood aside from his chosen profession and looked at it from outside.

chapter **I**

the ability to

criticize

and love

at the

same time

I had felt for some time that Catholicism in the United States was infantile. A child does not criticize his parents. He does not let others do so. As the child grows, he realizes the humanity of his parents, their objective vulnerability to criticism. This does not mean that the person loses love for his parents. Actually love should deepen as we realize what our parents have done for us. But the mature person can criticize what he loves, love what he criticizes.

When I was growing up one did not criticize the Church. One did not let others criticize — anybody or anything connected with the Church. The age was pockmarked with infantilism.

We have not grown into maturity as a Christian society. Not yet. In the past 10 years we have seen confusion, insecurity, questioning of everything. We have grown into . . . adolescence as a society. The pimples on our social face should surprise no one.

One thing about the virtue of adolescence: it is the threshold of maturity. When we finally arrive at the latter we will probably know — better than any society before us — what Christianity is all about.

The obvious question, "When will we finally get there?" is answered by the equally obvious, "When enough individuals have reached Christian maturity." A society is mature only when it contains sufficient numbers of mature individuals.

The answer has appalling overtones. So many things distract us from proper growth. No sooner has the post-Vatican furor begun to subside than we are confronted by "Jesus people," hippies, astrologists, witches, those interested in Oriental meditation, yoga, and emotionalism which is conveniently blamed on the Holy Spirit so that its proponents can hold their heads high against all audacious criticism. Will we ever get over our hangovers without running head-on into hang-ups by the binge-ful?

Such scamperings indicate the modern craving for . . . something. One might doubt that the craving is for authentic Christianity. The mainstream of Christianity has flowed — turbulently, messily, but with ever-living waters — for 20 centuries. If these eye-catching, if not popular, movements are not confluent with that mainstream, their proponents will continue to crave — for something — after their buzz is over. And Christian society will remain

adolescent. Mature Christian individuals have swum the mainstream down the ages. In those pre-Vatican, "static" years before the "emerging layman," Chesterton, Belloc, Waugh, Greene, Bloy, Mauriac and that liberated woman Undset sparkled in the field of literature. Unused to staring at their navels, much less picking at them, they crawled out of their doll houses and instead of brooding, contributed their talents to their times. Many of the challenges they met have changed in many ways. But the challenge to mature Christianity has not. It has become more poignant — perhaps more frustrating.

Francois Mauriac, Nobel Prize winner now enjoying his eternal Prize, was certainly not a member of the "modern" Church. But he was a mature Christian. And he could criticize.

His *Viper's Tangle* jostles us out of that old-time religion which saw everything as either black or white. His *Woman of the Pharisee* shows that being "right" is not always loving and therefore not always Christian. He did not hesitate to call the Roman Catholic Church the *Stumbling Block*.

And yet his criticism seems always to chal-

lenge the reader rather than to drown him in murky waters, as do the swamp-writers of so much modern literature. His criticisms were always balanced, always mature. They prodded to maturity. He was upset by the problem of too few Christians really being Christian, a phenomenon which seems to have eluded the most effective change-makers of our day.

> ' We must do the adversary this much justice. He seldom uses against us a weapon which we give him; he makes small use of the advantage he could take of us by showing us, without comment, the cross of which we unscrupulously boast . . . ' [1]

What kind of criticism is that? Old time? Christian? Is he really hitting us where it hurts? Bypassing superficialities, is he getting to meaty matters? Love and criticism are weeded in his work. His criticism comes out mature.

Leon Bloy criticized priests so much that one day someone asked how he could remain devotedly Catholic. He observed something to the effect that if he saw Peter

---

[1]F. Mauriac. *Stumbling Block*. Philosophical Library, (New York, 1952), p. 9.

denying our Lord he would have called down Peter with all his strength; but if Peter asked him to do one thing, he would do it without question. Here is maturity. Bloy saw the humanity in Peter. He loved it. He wanted it improved. He also saw the divinity in Peter. Hence, his total dedication.

Many in our Church today seem plagued by critical gastritis which manifests itself by broad, generalized negatives which are more of a belch than the product of reasoning. We have had mature individuals in the past, and have them now. We simply have not yet had enough to leaven society. It remains a fact that the *first characteristic of a mature Christian is that he can criticize maturely what he loves, loving what he criticizes.*

chapter II

seeing

things

in the

perspective

of the past

"What an appalling thought," I mused, when it dawned on me in my drab efficiency apartment. "As much as I have been disturbed by changes in the past decade, many people in the past century have had more reason to be shocked than I have now." This realization of the obvious affected me deeply, as the obvious budding into realization often does.

Only now are we popularly understanding what happened a hundred years ago. How many eons had Western man been agricultural? Probably back to the cave man. But with the coming of the industrial revolution things began to change. The pace was slow at first. But it progressed geometrically in the 20th century, so that now even the farmer must be a businessman in order to survive.

Despite the old dictum about Rome moving slowly, Pope Leo XIII picked up this radical change in our culture. He did not write before Karl Marx. But he wrote before any other leading Christian. This first pioneer social encyclical of his was called *Rerum Novarum,* which can be literally translated "Revolution." And with the publication of this encyclical the "modern Church" began.

Pope Leo denied nothing of authentic Christian tradition. He saw a changed world, went back to the old Gospel, and took from it a new insight needed for his time. He began to teach that to love Christ it was simply not enough to dole out new money and old clothes to the poor. The Christian should contribute toward a society in which every man has the opportunity to earn a decent living. This is what Leo presented to the world and what the official Church has been presenting right up to Vatican II — without prejudice to the authentically old in the Church's teachings.

And yet this Leonine doctrine was so shocking to the men of his time that some bishops of Latin America refused to publish it! What would have happened to Latin America, had they done so, staggers the imagination. But they weren't ready for it. The Pope's teaching was too new, too different.

Around 1910 Pope Pius X disturbed many Catholics by telling them they should receive Communion frequently! So you don't find that shocking? Well, in 1910 it was. In such awe of the divinity of Christ were the common Christians, that they stayed away from Communion except for once or twice a year. Pope Pius was asking

Christians to change their basic sacramental mentality. That sort of thing could be counted as much more significant than translating Mass language to the vernacular and turning the altar around. Pius X did not deny the divinity of Christ in the Blessed Sacrament, nor our need to show it reverence. He simply observed that Christ has made Himself available to us; and we should avail ourselves of Him — not because we are worthy, but because we need Him.

The Catholic of 1910 had to confront and cope with this dramatic change. We, in the seventies, should be upset?

Perhaps this man Pius should have been canonized on the sole fact that he began a revolution that has been progressing toward success ever since. For the liturgical changes that have affected us in the last decade are consonant with the aims of Pope Pius X. There *may* be greater esthetic beauty to the Latin liturgy. But the Latin Mass cannot hold a candle — even a liturgical one — to the vernacular Mass, if our purpose is to make the Sacraments more available to the people. That was the aim of Pius. It is the aim of the Church today in her official liturgical changes.

It is my further opinion that the changes which have affected us recently would have taken place even without Vatican II. All because of a man now pegged as arch-conservative, whose name was Pius XII.

I will never forget the pioneer American liturgist, Gerald Ellard, breathing a sigh of relief one day and ecstatically declaring, "Now we liturgists have a green light." He had just finished reading Pope Pius XII's encyclical *Mediator Dei.* Pius XII founded the Pontifical Biblical Institute in Rome, and he encouraged scholars in the field of Scripture — as well as other fields — fearlessly to pursue scientific truth. It was the same pope who preached a consciousness of community to the modern Catholic in his letter *Mystici Corporis.*

No one noticed that Pius XII was doing anything particularly new. As a matter of fact he wasn't. He was well within the realm of authentic Christian tradition. But he was taking the lid off things and laying the foundation upon which Vatican II could be built.

When Pope John proposed throwing open the windows of the Church, many of us got the uneasy feeling that something was badly wrong with the old structure. And

yet, interestingly enough, Pope John did not call in carpenters, plumbers, or union men. He called the bishops of the world, most of whom were conservative, all of whom had been trained in scholastic philosophy and theology. And the fresh air let in was not the heady stuff of existentialism, situation ethics, or modern Protestant thought. It was the fresh air of authentic Christianity. The theologians knew·Barth, Tillich, Brunner, and were no doubt influenced by them. But they also knew Newman, Moehler, Leo, both Pius X and XII, Adam, and the many men who have preached authentic Christianity to modern man. The fresh air was authentic Christianity.

There were cobwebs to be removed. "You have to go to confession before communion." "Kissing someone of the opposite sex for longer than three seconds will send you to hell." "Letting the Blessed Sacrament touch your teeth will discolor them." Such things one never found in the Baltimore Catechism. They were old wives' tales. They obstructed growth.

Vatican II did not deny authentic truths. Although the Baltimore Catechism may be a pedagogical anachronism, it can still be read without danger to faith! The danger in

its use is in our failing to see it for what it is: a skeleton on which flesh must grow. Vatican II made it easier for real living flesh to grow by popularizing the developments in authentic Christianity over the past hundred years or so. It gave us fresh insights into old truths as needed by our times.

This is the key to understanding what has been happening. It is Western culture that is changing. The Church is adapting, as a living organism should, to the changed atmosphere in which it must breathe.

I personally have misgivings in this area. But we must unveil those misgivings and see them for what they are: cultural rather than religious.

"While stands the coliseum ... " wrote Byron. With or without the coliseum, the Latin Rite has preserved the trappings of Roman culture down the centuries. It has been a reminder to us that we are Romans. And it is only when people are connected to their roots that they are strong.

"When Rome falls, the world." This is the thought that breeds misgivings in such as myself. Has the industrial revolution and the subsequent technological, urbanized

society made Roman culture obsolete? And if it has, can we survive? The Western World has adapted to many things through the centuries. But it has not done so without preserving the roots of its own culture.

The Roman Catholic Church has given cultural as well as religious service to Westerners down through the ages. Her rites have reminded us that we are Greco-Roman as well as Judeo-Christian.

chapter III

seeing things

in the

perspective

of the

present

It is only when we see things in the perspective of the past that we can hope for Christian maturity. We can understand the present with balance only when we see what has happened within authentic Christianity and in the world for the past hundred years.

But more is needed for maturity. We must also see things in the perspective of the present.

In the bayou country of South Louisiana (Grand Coteau) there is a lovely retreat house called "Our Lady of the Oaks." It was given to the Jesuit Fathers by the diocesan clergy as a centenary gift in 1938. Live oaks cast the peaceful atmosphere of the place. It is built in Spanish mission style. Four huge oaks grow in its patio.

Shortly after I arrived there recently, a good man came into my office. "Father," he said, "I am sick. I love this place. A miracle was worked for me on these grounds. I have brought fresh fish for a special dinner (Cajuns love to do that, bless them). But I can stay here no longer. And I will not return as long as that 'voodoo' thing is in your sanctuary."

What the man was referring to was a four-foot metal sculpture of Christ, knobbed head, mumified body, spindly arms reaching out from the sanctuary wall. So deep was the man's emotional disturbance that he felt the only thing for him to do was to leave.

Then I began to look around the place. There have been changes of improvement in the house since 1938. But I've heard no one lately criticizing the rubber pads on our kneelers, nor for that matter the air-conditioning. "You're making it too easy" is no longer a cry heard when the Church adapts physically to physical changes of the culture. Such changes do not disturb us.

I found few other changes outside this type in our retreat house. The trees are the same; the building, essentially the same. Stations of the Cross were still there — in three places. Rosary was still a part of our schedule.

The chapel itself was essentially unchanged. Stained-glass windows, which only a poor country pastor would buy, were still there. Modern carvings of our Lord and Lady were on either side of the chapel. They would offend no one — nor produce great

devotion either. It was all quite inoffensive — save *that*!

And what was *that*? It was a modern artist's attempt to "do his thing" for the modern Church! And here precisely is the eye of the hurricane for many modern Christians.

If the Church had not allowed the contemporary to "do his thing" for the contemporary Church, we would not have had an Aquinas, or a Palestrina, perhaps no Michelangelo. Creative people always make shock waves. And yet without them culture would be anemic.

The Church has given many innovators a hard time in ages past. But eventually those new thought and art forms which are good are accepted in Catholic circles. Teilhard de Chardin knew that. And he was smart enough to take steps to assure it. This must have contributed to his patient loyalty which the emulators of his "martyrdom" and thought should imitate.

In the past few years, the official Church has shown herself reluctant to crush the creative contemporary. I know some men who would have us get that Dutchman's thumb out of the dike so that we could flood the whole Dutch Church. And yet

the official Church does not follow such action or trend of thought. Perhaps she thinks we are adult enough, or educated enough, not to need the protections of the past. Or, too sophisticated to admit our need of them.

When the creative person has his day, we are bound to get some chaff along with the wheat. Our Lord said something about cutting the chaff and the wheat down too soon. If the official Church has finally tuned into that channel, far be it from me to blur the picture.

The fact that I can see a symbolism of Christ's love, His identification with corrupt humanity, His cross, His Church, His Incarnation, and His mother in that Grand Coteau piece does not mean that the sculpted image of our Christus is great. It only means I like it. I hope it lasts.

Yet I can appreciate the emotional disturbance in the man who rejected three days of grace, perhaps another miracle. When we are irritated by a shocking piece — no matter how creative — which occupies front and center of the stage, we are faced with a choice: either love it or leave it.

And the contributions of the contemporary

are front and center in Catholic life today. Hence, I can appreciate disturbed people leaving the visible Church.

My one hope is that they have enough honesty to admit that they are leaving because of a piece of fabricated tin! If they should take time and trouble to look around, they would see: the same creed, the same code (essentially), the same sacraments, the same pope, the same Church which have existed in the mainstream for nearly two thousand years.

chapter **IV**

arrival

at maturity:

seeing

the essence of

the good news

And this brings us to the culminating characteristic of the mature Christian: to see the essence of Christianity and to be able to distinguish it from the accidentals.

On that night of nights many centuries ago, an angel announced to simple, unlearned shepherds the "Good News." And they understood it.

I wonder if any one of us could state the "Good News" in terms simple enough for shepherds today? Or would we have to send them packing to 12 years of CCD?

One day while meditating, Ignatian contemplation completely enraptured me. (Those who have made Jesuit retreats will understand.) The idea is just to stare at, become a part of a scene of our Lord's life as one would stare at and become part of a beautiful sunrise or mountain scene.

I was at the River Jordan. Our Lord came to be baptized. After a bit of bickering over his own unworthiness, John poured the water as Jesus stood in the Jordan. Our Lord became identified with sinful human nature. At that moment, the Holy Spirit descended on our Lord in the form of a dove. And a voice came from heaven. "This is my beloved Son. Hear Him."

I have had only rare success with Ignatian contemplation. But at this instant, conviction came like an April day. "This is it," I thought to myself. So graphic was my mental picture of the scene.

Man has been so fouled up in his quest of God. It has at times been a nagging quest, producing many weird concepts.

If we might follow for the moment Erich Fromm's evolutionary theory of religion as given in *The Art of Loving*, primitive man first felt a need to be accepted by the nature to which he was so close. And so he developed nature gods, totems, etc.

But this was not enough. He needed to feel accepted for himself by another person. Who else but a mother? And so he developed mother deities. Since this led to a kind of imbalance, he then developed a father god, one who would reward good and punish evil — a dire god of sanction. Then, in need of protection in all facets of life, he developed the many different gods which we see exemplified in the cultures of Egypt, Greece and Rome.

Next came the god of Aristotle (reason) which the West made abominable by taking it too seriously: The immanent, tran-

scendent, never-changing, ever-present, all-powerful one, whose greatest triumph has been in giving the West (strangely not the East) an unrelievable headache over such things as predestination, freedom, grace, and the very goodness of God.

Finally, Jesus came. As a climax of the revelations given through Judaism, He sweeps aside all these god-concepts. Very graphically at the Jordan, He is telling us, "God is not merely the Father of sanction (which of course He is, however much we moderns want to play the ostrich), but also the Father of compassion, the Father of the prodigal son. But He is more. God is Son, therefore my brother who has called me friend. And yet still more. God is also Spirit, the sort of thing that we breathe in and which, though elusive, is the thing that gives life. He is *ruah* which is biblical Hebrew for the life-sustaining Breath of man."

Mere words cannot convey this beauty, but contemplation on the baptism of Christ can bring us closer to this astounding truth. Words cannot say it as beautifully as a humble baptism. If we concentrate on His baptism as though staring over peaceful lake waters, we will find a concept of God more beautiful than any man has ever con-

ceived or could conceive.

Theologians may examine the Blessed Trinity in their analytical laboratory; but they will find, like biologists, only a dead frog if they take themselves too seriously.

The fact is that our Lord warned us that no one knows God except the One who has descended from above and those to whom He reveals himself. And He who has descended has graphically said: God is Father; God is Son, our Brother; God is Spirit, the sustainer of life.

But the "Good News" goes further yet.

One Christmas day I found myself discussing with a four-year-old boy the beauties of life that would unfold for him. Perhaps he'd shoulder a fishing pole one day and go down to the creek with his father. He'd throw in the line, get his first bite, his first fish, and be thrilled with it all. He'd find a new dimension to life, a new depth.

Later, he might find a friend, the type to share things with, to play marbles with, etc. Again, a new dimension, a new richness. Then some day he'd look into the eyes of a woman and find out what a deep relationship between man and woman really is. A

new dimension. A new richness.

But no matter how many experiences un-folded for him — giving new dimensions, new richness — the main dimension of his life, the one which gives him his essential richness, the young four year old already had. He had been baptized.

According to the revelation of Jesus Christ, those in grace share the triune life of God — like husbands and wives share each other's lives. This means that if I can think of one deep moment of union between two persons — say, the deepest moment of union between husband and wife — such a union I have with God! Mind you, I do not feel the ecstasy of that union. *That* is what heaven's all about. But in the meantime, the actual relationship between God and myself when I am, as Paul says, in Christ, is like that of spouse to spouse in their deep-est moment of union!

Unbelievable? It is not my thought. It is the Good News of Jesus Christ. God is Father, Son, Spirit. And He shares His life with me.

And that is the essence of Christianity. The Church — with its laws and hierarchy, with its changes and reluctance to change, with

its popes and cardinals, hospital nuns and missionary brothers, its structures, its doctrines, its adaptability — is simply the servant of that Good News. It has always been thus — through the turbulence and changes of two thousand years of mainstream Christianity.

epilogue

When one wends his way back to the ministry, it is through the forest — with its darkness, its tigers, its lotus blossoms. He knows
that he does not have to give up a wife,
family, intimacy to live the Good News. He
knows that when he comes home to the
vows he will find the same road, to be
traveled by the same person.

Human love is such today that one finds
sympathy when one veers from the path in
search of greater happiness, greater fulfillment. But human love is not so understanding, I have found, to such sentiments as: "I
will return to my original commitment. I
will resume my chosen path."

Human love is the lotus blossom. I do not
know whether lotus blossoms can be
turned into orchids or, if you will, American Beauty roses. But in Christ, God
breathes divine love into human love. And
what results is the most beautiful thing the
world has ever seen.

As long as the Church requires thorough
commitment of her ministers, there must

be those who are dedicated to teaching the perspective of past and present, and in that context spreading the Good News. This dedication will keep priests faithful — no matter how many detours or failures. This perspective will make Christians mature — and will make human love divine.